Emotional
Intelligence

A Guide To Managing And Understanding
Emotions Within Yourself And Others To
Achieve Happiness, Great Relationships
And Success In Life!

By Mark West

I0412898

Table of Contents

Introduction...4

Chapter 1-What Is Emotional Intelligence?....... 8

Chapter 2-IQ versus EI: Battle of the Intelligences..21

Chapter 3-How Do You Measure Emotional Intelligence? 32

Chapter 4-What the Professionals Say 36

Chapter 5-IQ meets EI: A Marriage Of Convenience.. 42

Chapter 6-Applying Emotional Intelligence In Your Life 51

Chapter 7-Using Emotional Intelligence in Your Dealings with Others.. 63

Conclusion 75

Introduction

If you could have any superpower, what would it be? As cliché as this question is, it gets some interesting answers. Some people want to fly-that is a big one-, some people want to see through walls-or clothes-, and some people want the ability to control the weather-or bend steel.

Interestingly enough, another common answer that you will get to this question, is the ability to read other people's minds. This is not surprising though, when you think of the advantages of having this skill. You will be able to foresee how other people will react in certain situations, or you will be able to pre-empt questions and attitudes, and give a more focused and measured response.

Reading other people's minds however, is not really a superpower. It is a skill that you can develop with time and commitment; a skill that you can hone with the direct application of a few important variables. That is where Emotional Intelligence comes into play!

Emotional Intelligence, or EI, is a fairly new field when compared to its more scientific brother, IQ. It has been investigated at length, from around the 1930s, and has gone through several crises of identity, being called everything from 'social intelligence' by Edward Thorndike, to the 'emotional quotient' by Keith Beasley (although EI and the emotional quotient have since been given different identities). Whatever you call it, it has come to be an important element of intelligence, one that cannot be ignored today by anybody who is serious about his or her life.

Having an applied knowledge of how EI works is therefore a critical skill. It is essential that you understand not only your own emotions, but also the emotions of others, if you are to navigate your way to successful living. Your interpersonal relationships, working relationships, and your relationship with yourself can all benefit greatly from an intimate understanding of Emotional Intelligence.

So, how do you get to grips with your own emotions, and how do you learn to read those of other people? What are the benefits of applying this newfound skill in the real world, and how does this help you to navigate the sometimes-rocky terrain of personal relationships? How can Emotional Intelligence lead to success in every sphere of your life?

Before we answer all these questions, one question begs our attention though. Just what is Emotional Intelligence?

The information that follows will give you an insight into the world of Emotional Intelligence, its applications, and how you can learn and develop this skill. You will come to realize the importance of EI, and you will be equipped with the skills necessary to work your way successfully out of any situation.

Getting to grips with this knowledge is a formidable tool to have in your psychological armory. Developing your EI muscle will serve you well in your pursuit of success in any arena of your life. And the more you use it, the stronger this muscle will become.

But let us not get ahead of ourselves. Let us start with the first question on your mind, and answer that question completely. Then we will work through some situations in your life that you might find yourself in. We will learn how the application of EI can help you to work through these painlessly.

So, just what is Emotional Intelligence?

Chapter 1-What Is Emotional Intelligence?

Imagine you arrive early for work. You go straight to the coffee station for your morning fix, and you hear sobbing coming from the corner. Instinct tells you to go over and put an arm on your colleague's shoulder, and tell them the generic 'whatever it is, it cannot be that bad, everything is going to be okay!' You are careful though, not wanting to invade someone else's private space, or become involved in whatever moment they're having.

Or what if you are at your desk, and you look up to see your boss standing there, smoke coming out of his ears. He comes down on you hard, and then storms off in a huff, leaving you confused and wondering what exactly just happened. You see the files that have been placed on your desk, some which are largely unrelated to your function in the organization's operations. You wonder where this attack came from so suddenly.

Imagine you are out for drinks with friends, and you notice that somebody is watching you from across the bar. Everything inside you says that you should go over and say hello, but every book that you have read has advised you to play it cool, and to let them come to you. So you continue pretending not to see them watching you. You continue to pretend not to be watching them. Until eventually they just get up and move on.

How do you traverse a world with so many emotions being thrown at you every day, with no clear indication as to how to respond to them? What do you do in order not to make a fool of yourself, or expose yourself to rejection? How do you preserve your already fragile ego from the pain of this rejection?

Now, think of all the goals that you have ever set for yourself. How many of these have you actually achieved? What is it that has held you back from realizing your dreams, and reaching your full potential? Just how much of what you achieve-or do not achieve-is dependent on you having an above average IQ?

At some point in your life-preferably sooner rather than later-you will ask yourself at least a few of these questions. If you are lucky, then you will have explored your own limitations constructively, with a view to finding a solid way forward. Even if you have not done this yet, however, the best time to do this-if you have not achieved the success you dream of-is right now!

Having a high IQ does not guarantee that you will make it in life. In fact, being academically inclined is usually the first step on a road to becoming a certified hermit. Granted, you stand a better chance of earning six figures with a good education, and your best chance of receiving this education is with an above average IQ, but this is not a guarantee that you will be happy.

You will need to be in tune with other aspects of your intelligence, if you are to have any hope of making a complete success of your life. You must be in touch with your emotions, in control of them, and have the ability to understand and manipulate the emotions of others. This Emotional Intelligence is what will ensure that you make it in this world, or at least provide you with a clear roadmap towards this success.

Relationships, happiness, and overall success are within your reach. All you have to do is apply yourself to the development of your Emotional Intelligence muscle, until you can read yourself and others, the same way you read a book, the newspaper, or a magazine. Emotional Intelligence is a critical component to your overall development.

So, Just What Is Emotional Intelligence?

In a leading article titled '*Emotional Intelligence*', Peter Salovey and John D. Mayer describe Emotional Intelligence as '*the subset of social intelligence that involves the ability to monitor one's own and others' feelings and emotions, to discriminate among them and use this information to guide one's thinking and actions.*'

The ability to perceive emotions is considered a 'soft skill'. This is because it falls outside the ambit of scientific quantification; therefore, it falls just shy of the esteem bestowed upon the hard sciences. If you have a high IQ, for instance, then you 'know' that you are smart. Given the tests that measure the Intelligence Quotient, they render the results as a reliable indicator of one's intellectual aptitude.

Emotional Intelligence is different. Being able to control your emotions and to evaluate the emotions of others might not be as clearly definable, but it is no less important than IQ. Researchers have actually suggested that EI (Emotional Intelligence) is more important than IQ.

Here Is Why!

Richard Branson was intellectually challenged, by modern conventions. He had difficulty reading, and understanding math problems that some of us would consider basic. As a dyslexic young man, Richard cannot be said to have had a high IQ. In fact, it can be said that his IQ was lower than average.

However, Richard Branson is one of the wealthiest men alive today! His Virgin Group has over 400 companies in its stable. In fact, it was his headmaster who said to him that he would either end up in prison, or become a millionaire. Sir Richard Branson is a billionaire today!

To sum up his character, in his autobiography, Branson is quoted as saying, about his decision to start an airline, "*My interest in life comes from setting myself huge, apparently unachievable challenges and trying to rise above them...from the perspective of wanting to live life to the full, I felt I had to attempt it!*"

He had a resilience that paid off in dividends. This never-say-die attitude has stood him apart from his contemporaries, and it is a trait that he has been working on his whole life. Success did not come easy for this billionaire, and still it is not guaranteed that everything he touches turns to instant gold. But when he believes in something, there is very little that distracts him from his ultimate goal.

Now, before you make all those self-righteous proclamations about how money isn't everything, and how you would be satisfied with just enough, think of this:

- Richard Branson runs several companies across the world, with a very happy staff contingent.
- He gets to vacation with his family, spend time with his wife, and has had the luxury of watching his children grow up because he has never had to keep office hours.
- He gets to do things that he is passionate about-like flying a hot-air balloon around the world or scuba diving in the Great Barrier Reef-with little concern for his bottom line, because his companies basically run themselves.
- Richard Branson is fulfilled in every aspect of his life, and can be considered happy by any standard.

And he achieved all this, and continues to achieve great things, all with a below than average IQ. This man is not driven by money, either. He is not motivated by making more of it. He has a genuine curiosity, and he seeks to satisfy his innate curiosity in every aspect of his life. All this from someone who showed poor academic performance.

What Richard Branson has is an incredibly high EI, or Emotional Intelligence! This can be seen in how he has managed his personal and professional relationships. Reading any one of his many biographical works, you get an intimate insight into the man behind the Virgin Empire. You get a look into the inner workings of this great man, and you can understand why he has managed to become so successful.

It has been suggested that Emotional Intelligence is a quality that can be learned and strengthened. Some researchers however, claim that this is a characteristic that you are born with, and that some have it, while others simply do not. Considering the four factors of Emotional Intelligence, as suggested by the Salovey and Mayer model, it can however be argued that indeed, this is a characteristic that one can develop with time and practice.

What Are These Four Branches Of Emotional Intelligence?

1. **Perceiving Emotions**: When it comes to understanding emotions, the first step is to develop the ability to perceive them. Body language and facial expressions are nonverbal signals that you should be able to read and understand if you are to make an accurate assessment of how another person is feeling.

2. **Reasoning With Emotions**: The second step is to use emotions to promote thinking and cognitive activity. We use emotion to give priority to what we pay attention to, and what we react to. When something captures our attention, we respond to it emotionally.

3. **Understanding Emotions:** Why is the person that you are interacting with so angry? What is the underlying cause of this anger, and what does it mean for you in the interaction? The emotions that you perceive can carry a variety of meanings, so it is important that you understand the why behind the what!

4. **Managing Emotions:** Managing emotions effectively is a critical component of Emotional Intelligence. You need to be able to regulate emotions, respond appropriately, and respond accordingly to the emotions of others. These are all important aspects of emotional management.

The four components of Emotional Intelligence above sum up perfectly what EI is. Other factors contribute to the strengthening of this skill, however; but when it comes to the development of this characteristic, the above encapsulate all the important aspects of Emotional Intelligence.

How though, can you benefit from the application of Emotional Intelligence?

Here Is How!

Having the ability to identify emotions and to use them effectively can be very beneficial to you. Having the ability to understand and manage emotions in positive ways can produce great results in every aspect of your life. One of the most significant benefits of applying EI is the relief of stress. You will be able to see situations as they develop and chart an appropriate way forward.

Another benefit is the ability to communicate effectively. This not only helps you in negotiations, but it goes a very long way in diffusing conflicts that may arise in your home or work life. This is because it helps you to understand where the other person is coming from, and how best to utilize the emotions within yourself to move any situation forward.

You will be able to show empathy for other people, and you will be able to overcome any difficulty in your way. With the many aspects of your life that are impacted on by your use of Emotional Intelligence, how you behave and how you interact with other people are probably the most defining.

In 1995, psychologist and New York Times science writer Daniel Goleman wrote a book entitled '*Emotional Intelligence: Why It Can Matter More Than IQ*!' This benchmark piece of literature outlines the importance of Emotional Intelligence, and plays it up against its more scientific counterpart, IQ. What this book reveals to us, is that EI can, and probably is more important to the overall development of the individual.

Just how different are these two intelligences, however. How do they compare with one another, and is this even a fair comparison? Let us now compare these two very different and very specific character traits, and see which one comes up tops!

Chapter 2-IQ versus EI: Battle of the Intelligences

What is the difference between the Intelligence Quotient and the Emotional Quotient? Basically, it is the part of a person's mental abilities that they measure. IQ is a measure of how well a person is able to understand information, while EI measures how well a person understands emotion.

The Emotional Quotient measures how one recognizes emotions within themselves and others. It is also how well a person manages these emotions, making them more efficient when working in groups, or even alone. IQ gives an indication of one's ability to learn, understand and apply information in a meaningful way. This is the major difference between EI and IQ.

Which of these two is more important to achieving success in your life or your career?

Granted, both are instrumental in assuring happiness and your ability to succeed. However, EI is more difficult to live without. IQ definitely has its advantages and affords you opportunities that would be seriously lacking if you had a lower than average IQ. However, Emotional Intelligence carries a lot more weight.

This is because we are social creatures. We interact with one another every day in a number of situations from our emotional centers, and not from our intellect. People are very different, and we have varying degrees of intelligence, so we need a strong EI if we are to deal effectively with these varying levels of intelligence.

Take the following example:

You have a manager of a team of general workers. The manager has an average IQ, but knows how to do his job very well. His team, however, is made up of a melting pot of characters. Some of them are focused and calm, others are highly strung and emotionally unstable. One of them has a drinking problem, and another one is on the verge of divorce. And one of them has a child with developmental problems.

A competent manager would ask himself whether each of his team members were able to carry out their designated functions, so that targets are met and productivity does not suffer. He or she would not focus on the team's personal lives, provided they delivered on their jobs. If their work suffered, the manager would call in the specific team member involved, and address the issue related to their performance.

Chances are the team member would say that they are sorry, and that it will never happen again. They might blame the equipment or a supervisor. Instinctively, they will not own their part in the problem, and the manager will be left less than satisfied that the problem has been resolved.

The team member in question might walk away feeling attacked. They might ask themselves questions along the lines of 'why does my boss not understand that I'm going through stuff?', or 'why is it always me, why can I never do anything right?' The manager might walk away feeling dismissed, and asking himself why the employee did not see that the problem was of his or her own making.

No amount of IQ will resolve this situation. There is no way that either party involved will reach a solution that will lead to improved productivity on the part of the employee and the manager will still not reach their targets. Understanding information will definitely not serve any of them.

An astute manager, one with a high EI, will look deeper at the situation. They will ask the right questions, and not just scratch the superficial surface of the problem. They will want to know what is going on in the employee's personal life (not necessarily their private lives) that could lead to such a drastic dip in their performance. They will explore the emotions involved in an attempt to get to the root of the problem.

Now, professional lines are there for a reason. This does not mean that you cannot, and should not traverse this line if it means that productivity suffers. EI is a measure of how well you can understand and disseminate emotions, in yourself and in others, so that you can work better as a team. Sometimes this involves getting involved personally in the lives of your employees, so that you can understand what drives them, what motivates them, and what drives them crazy.

The above example might be very basic, but it suggests unequivocally that EI is more important than IQ. It displays how people with a higher EI do not necessarily have to have a high IQ to achieve good results, at work, or in life. This is because social skills, and not technical knowledge, are what we use in our everyday lives. While people with high IQs might be good at understanding information, they may find it difficult to make themselves understood on a real human level.

An article in Forbes said, *"Research carried out by the Carnegie Institute of Technology shows that 85% of your financial success is due to skills in "human engineering," your personality, and ability to communicate, negotiate, and lead. Shockingly, only 15% is due to technical knowledge. Additionally, Israeli-American psychologist Daniel Kahneman, found that people would rather do business with a person they like and trust rather than someone they don't, even if the likable person is offering a lower quality product or service at a higher price."*

EI is therefore better at indicating success in the workplace. It is used to identify leaders, good team players, and people who work best by themselves. This is important if you are to make a success of the team that you manage. You will be able to assign people tasks best suited to their personalities, and you will be able to move them between tasks because of your ability to constantly re-evaluate their shifting emotions.

Entrepreneurs benefit greatly from having a high Emotional Intelligence as well. You will know what drives and motivates you on an individual level, and also have an intimate understanding of your ability to work well with other people. If people are not your thing mind you, you will know this from your understanding of your own emotional makeup.

On the one hand, IQ gives an indication of how good an individual is at challenging tasks. It shows ability to analyze information and to use that information to paint a picture that makes sense. With a high IQ, you will likely have great research capabilities and you will be able to develop strategies based on this research.

On the other hand, it identifies individuals with special needs, or those who face mental challenges. If you fall in this group, you are considered to have a low IQ, and your chances of succeeding academically are limited. Can you develop your IQ, however, so that you increase your chances of academic success? Research suggests that you cannot.

Emotional Intelligence is different. In the workplace, people with a high EI tend to fall easily into positions of leadership. They display impeccable teamwork capabilities, successful inter-personal relations, initiative and collaboration. You can identify those who work best alone, as well as those who have social challenges that make it difficult for them to operate in groups or teams.

The tests for IQ are relatively standardized, so you can either do them or you cannot. Emotional Intelligence is far more forgiving, and while they are still striving for standardized tests for EI, the skills involved in having a high Emotional Intelligence are easier to develop and strengthen. This is good news for the majority of the population, many of us just bordering on average IQs.

In business, you are always looking for the competitive edge. People have always thought that hiring smart intellectuals was the way to gain this advantage. More and more though, people are realizing that high IQs do not always translate to great job performance. While cognitive ability is good to have, the fact that it does not change much after 12 or 15 years of age means that it is a very limiting indicator of a person's ability in the workplace.

Good decision-making requires more than just intellect. People who succeed do so by building relationships, recognizing their own emotions, responding to the needs of others, and by revealing their own mistakes. This is what has become known as Emotional Intelligence, and this is a characteristic that can be learned. That is great news for the population.

People with higher EIs tend to be more optimistic. They have the ability to anticipate the best possible outcomes for actions or events. They are also extremely self-aware, with an intimate knowledge of their current emotional state, strengths, and weaknesses. They are empathetic, and understand other's viewpoints and the decision-making processes. They are also able to mitigate the urge to act, thinking first, controlling the impulse to act, and then acting accordingly.

With the ability to see things as they are, not as they want them to be, people with higher EIs are better equipped to be good leaders. While some managers can go on to become great leaders, some of them only ever remain good managers. You can also apply this in your private life, more so even than in the workplace.

How So?

Being able to identify, either by body language or facial expression, that your partner as not having a good day, you will know that you need to handle them with care. With the ability to read the signs of another's emotions, you can plot a course to deal with them, and make them more comfortable in the interaction.

So, we know that IQ is measured by standardized tests, but just how do you measure Emotional Intelligence. Considered a soft skill, there are considerably more variables associated with EI, which might make it difficult to measure. However, researchers have worked diligently to develop these tools to give you an indication of where you are at with regards to your Emotional Intelligence. You will know what you need to work on, and how you need to apply yourself to strengthen this muscle.

There have been a number of tools developed to measure Emotional Intelligence. The following is a discussion of some of these methods of testing; and how you can work at developing this skill in your own life.

Chapter 3-How Do You Measure Emotional Intelligence?

Psychological tests have a bad reputation. With everyone being so unique, that we would use a fixed set of criteria to determine aspects of a person's personality seems absurd. In fact, many people find it problematic that you would assign a number to an emotion-related quality like Emotional Intelligence.

Some have suggested that to measure or categorize us, would be to equate us to a commodity or an object. This debate can become very sensitive, many people being offended that they can be classified like a thing in a store, or a bag of groceries. With banks, the government and even supermarkets already treating us like numbers, do we really need psychologists buying into this as well?

We need to remember however, that self-knowledge is a core human value. And how can we ever hope to understand ourselves without some form of independent feedback? As far as this feedback is concerned, psychological tests are among the most impartial, accurate, and efficient means for discovering a person's attributes. When used with respect for the individual, they can prove to be invaluable aids to self-discovery and self-understanding.

Now, there have been many tests developed over the last couple of years that claim to evaluate Emotional Intelligence, but few that are backed up by substantial research. Here is a brief discussion of those tests with at least five published journal articles that provide empirical data based on the test.

- **Reuven Bar-On's EQ-i**

This is a self-report test that is designed to measure various competencies. These include stress tolerance, awareness, problem solving and happiness. According to Bar-On, *"Emotional Intelligence is an array of noncognitive capabilities, competencies and skills that influence a person's ability to succeed in coping with environmental demands and pressures."*

- **Emotional Competence Inventory (ECI)**

Based on an instrument known as the Self-Assessment Questionnaire, the ECI involves getting people who know the individual to offer ratings of that person's abilities on a number of different emotional competencies.

- **Multifactor Emotional Intelligence Scale (MEIS)**

An ability-based test in which the individual performs tasks designed to assess their ability to perceive, identify, understand and utilize emotions.

- **Seligman Attributional Style Questionnaire (SASQ)**

This test measures optimism and pessimism. It was originally designed as a screening test for Metropolitan Life, the insurance company.

- **The Mayer-Salovey-Caruso Emotional Intelligence Test (MSCEIT)**

This test is also an ability-based test designed to measure the four branches of the EI model of Mayer and Salovey. It was developed from an intelligence testing tradition formed by the emerging scientific understanding of emotions and their function and from the first published ability measure specifically intended to measure Emotional Intelligence. This was known as the Multifactor Emotional Intelligence Scale.

These tests contain scales and subscales, and you will receive a score for each one. You will also receive a score for your overall EQ. They vary in length and involvement, but the general idea of each one is the same. Your score will give you an understanding of how well developed you are in this area of intelligence.

Chapter 4-What the Professionals Say

A wide variety of factors plays a role in the success of any business venture today. One of these factors has gone largely unnoticed for a very long time. Fortunately however, this has changed over the last while. Emotional Intelligence has gained popularity as an essential skill that one needs to have if one is to succeed in business.

The same can be said for family life, or school life. In fact, almost every aspect of your life is affected by your ability to understand emotions within yourself and others, and to respond to these emotions accordingly. This is why EI is crucial if you are to enjoy success in every aspect of your life.

From as early as the 1930s, professionals have had an opinion surrounding Emotional Intelligence. Some of these have been negative, but mostly they have been advocates for EI, based on years of personal research, and an understanding of its importance.

Often called the father of modern educational psychology, Edward Lee Thorndike was one of the first professionals to allude to Emotional Intelligence in the 1930s. Referring to it as *'social intelligence'*, Thorndike described it as the ability to get along with people. It was ground breaking at its first mention, but his statement soon gained some serious traction.

In the 1940s, David Wechsler suggested that affective components of intelligence might be essential for success in every aspect of life. This has proven true, more than even he could have imagined. The impact of Emotional Intelligence on one's life cannot be denied, and the lack thereof has proven since he said it, to be detrimental.

The suggestion that you can actually build your emotional strength was made by psychologists like Abraham Maslow, as early as the 1950s. This added a level to Emotional Intelligence that was as intriguing in concept as it was in its application. People started to accept that unlike IQ, EI was something that could be worked on and strengthened over time.

This was further expanded upon in 1975, with the publication of *The Shattered Mind* by Howard Gardner. In this work, Gardner put forward the suggestion of multiple intelligences. While this was by no means a new study, it is said to be the first time that someone actually articulated it.

It was in 1985 however, that Wayne Payne first introduced the term 'Emotional Intelligence'. He did this in his doctoral dissertation entitled "*A study of emotion: developing emotional intelligence; self-integration; relating to fear, pain and desire (theory, structure of reality, problem-solving, contraction/expansion, tuning in/coming out/letting go).*"

While Reuven Bar-On claimed to have used the term 'emotional quotient' in an unpublished version of his graduate thesis, the first published use of the term was in a 1987 article in Mensa Magazine by Keith Beasley. This is not to be confused with EI (Emotional Intelligence) mind you, but it certainly is an expansion on the theme. Where IQ is a measure of intelligence, EQ or the Emotional Quotient is a measure of Emotional Intelligence.

Peter Salovey and John Mayer, in their 1990 article '*Emotional Intelligence*', which was published in the journal *Imagination, Cognition and Personality* became a model for the study and application of Emotional Intelligence. This was a landmark article in every sense of the word, and the pair went on to develop the Mayer-Salovey-Caruso Emotional Intelligence Test.

Interestingly, John Mayer also developed the Systems Framework For Personal Psychology, and authored *Personal Intelligence: The Power Of Personality And How It Shapes Our Lives*! Peter Salovey has served on the National Science Foundation's Social Psychology Advisory Panel,

the National Institute Of Mental Health
Behavioral Science Working Group, and the
NIMH National Advisory Mental Health Council.

Daniel Goleman however, popularized the term
'Emotional Intelligence'. He is a psychologist and
New York Times science writer, and in 1995, he
published a book called *Emotional Intelligence:
Why It Can Matter More Than IQ*! This book
served to solidify EI as a field of psychology to be
taken seriously. Comparing it to IQ held it up to
scrutiny by the scientific fraternity and
established it once and for all in the minds of
many as a science.

Many pieces have subsequently been written
about Emotional Intelligence. These have added
to the work previously presented, and built on
the foundations that had been laid by
professionals before. What all these
professionals are in agreement of though, is that
Emotional Intelligence has a definite place in the
psychological makeup of human beings, and that

it serves us greatly in our endeavor for success and living a balanced life.

The suggestion by Goleman, that Emotional Intelligence might be more important than IQ, raised more than a few eyebrows. But to suggest that one exists separately from the other, or that one is not directly proportional to the other, is a little ambitious.

Or is it?

Can Emotional Intelligence exist independently of IQ? How can these two seemingly opposing ideas marry together to increase the individual's chances of successful living? Why is it that people with higher IQs tend to lack the ability to adequately express themselves on an emotional level? Are these two concepts directly or inversely proportional to one another? Are they related at all?

These questions will be explored in the following chapter.

Chapter 5-IQ meets EI: A Marriage Of Convenience

The Intelligence Quotient has long been the gold standard in measures of mental capabilities. It has been argued that people with higher IQs stand a better chance of success in life, and therefore they are happier. This has proven not to be the case, and it has been discovered that human beings actually have a number of intelligences, all contributing in their own way to overall happiness.

Emotional Intelligence has taken over as the most fundamental characteristic that serves as a precursor to happiness, however. People with high EIs tend to be happier and more successful than their counterparts who are 'limited' by a high IQ. This lends credence to the suggestion by Goleman that Emotional Intelligence is in fact more important than IQ.

Can these two concepts exist separately however, seemingly isolated from one another?

In a word, yes! The reason for this is that they measure two very different characteristics. One measures your ability to learn, to understand and analyze information, to connect the dots. The other is a measure of emotional understanding, both of the self and of others. It is the extent to which you can perceive, understand and respond to emotions, and the extent to which you can choose to act-or not to act-accordingly.

Therefore, Emotional Intelligence can exist independently of IQ! A person with a high IQ can be seen to have a lower level of Emotional Intelligence, and vice versa. Both concepts stand up in the face of very specific scrutiny, individual to each one, so that comparing them would be like comparing apples and oranges. Can they, however, coexist in the same space? Can these two seemingly opposing ideas marry together to increase the individual's chances of successful living?

The answer to this question too, is yes! While people with higher IQs tend to have difficulty with getting people to understand them, that is not to say that they are happy with being that way. In fact, feelings of being misunderstood abound among the intellectually inclined, so that they flock together in order to establish safety in numbers.

But safety from what?

Well, safety from the scrutiny that leaves the rest of us vulnerable in social contexts. Even in the workplace, the higher up the ladder you go, the lonelier it gets. This is mostly in cases where a high IQ is a prerequisite for position. This prerequisite no longer qualifies, needless to say, at least not exclusively in most instances, and not anymore.

Consider this:

The CEO of a major financial group has the perfect resume. She works twelve hours a day, always the first to arrive, and always the last to leave. She has an IQ that is considered way above average, and she knows this. This is the part of her that she identifies with. She has made everything in her life about what she knows.

She does all this while juggling the pressures of raising a family. One of her children is about to go off to college, and the other is entering puberty. Her husband is sleeping with his secretary. Needless to say, her family life is suffering, and is on the brink of falling apart completely. In fact, you could say that it already has.

Commitment to her work is all she has to look forward to these days. It is the all-encompassing driving force behind her life. She tries to spend as much time at the office as possible, not realizing that she has missed watching her young adult growing up, and not noticing that her teenager really needs her. Her husband sought comfort in another woman's arms because she was never around, always busy, and always tired.

Not that there is any excuse for infidelity, but had the CEO in the above example managed her time better, then she would not have missed out on so many birthdays, and she might have been a little more present for her husband. Her family life, and in essence, her private life, need not have suffered on the altar of career advancement. All the while, the CEO seems blissfully unaware of what is going on, on the home front.

Or maybe she is aware. Maybe she just assumes that she will sort out her home life once she has closed the next big deal, or once things 'normalize' at work. This example might seem extreme, but many people today go through this on some level or another. Many people are affected by the ambitions of the ones they love, usually to their detriment.

Time Management is not the only problem faced by the CEO, however. It is a symptom of a far deeper problem. Just what is that problem? What could our CEO have done differently, and still achieved the secular success she so desperately needs and wants?

Well, having a low Emotional Intelligence is the leading factor in not living a balanced life. Before you ask yourself how someone so 'intelligent' can be so dumb, consider the following:

- The burden of being 'clever' has a very powerful influence on the way we act.
- We ignore emotions in our pursuit to be right.
- The higher your IQ, the more you feel you need to show the world the substance of the grey matter between your ears.
- We often put the development of our Emotional Intelligence on the back burner while we pursue positions that we think will fulfill us.

The CEO in the above example is in no way a lost cause, mind you. She just needs to take a few steps back in order to restore balance to her life and make significant strides in all aspects of her existence.

How So?

A key component of Emotional Intelligence is self-awareness. 'Know thyself' is an adage as old as time, because it rings very true for every individual. It is a classic theme in life, and what we know about classics is that they do not change. Our CEO therefore needs to take the time out for some serious introspection.

Questions that she should ask herself are why I feel the need to achieve the things I strive for, what motivates the choices that I make, and the ones that I have made in my life? Other questions include why my family is important to me, why is my work important to me, and how do I feel about the various areas in my life?

These will give the CEO some insight into the key drivers in her life. These are very personal questions, and they serve the purpose of reintroducing the individual to themselves.

There are many other questions that the CEO could-and should-ask, but the questions above are a good start.

Once the CEO has become more self-aware, a process that could take some time, she will be in a better position to start developing her Emotional Intelligence. This is just the first step in a long road, but the rewards at the end of this journey are many and incredible.

While IQ is a given, Emotional Intelligence is not. It is something that you need to work on over time until your EI is sufficiently developed so that you see positive changes start to occur in your life.

IQ and EI are as different as night and day. But they can coexist in the same mind. We are social creatures who constantly interact with one another. These interactions could be beneficial or detrimental. This depends largely on how Emotionally Intelligent you are.

So just how do you apply Emotional Intelligence In Your Life? How can this benefit you in practically every area of your existence?

Chapter 6-Applying Emotional Intelligence In Your Life

How well do you resolve conflict? Are you always creating conflict? How are you at anger management? How well do you deal with adversity?

Are you quick to give criticism? How well do you take it? Are you an effective problem solver? Can you motivate yourself? How do you respond to the feelings and emotions of others?

These questions get to the heart of Emotional Intelligence. Answering them honestly, you will start to get to the meat of your EI muscle, and start to develop it. Other questions are:

- How comfortable, if at all, are you in exchanging your thoughts and feelings with your intimate partner, or with your family?

- Can you build cooperative relationships, or are most of your relationships destructive?
- How do you deal with difficult people; do you blame them for being difficult; or are you self-aware enough to realize that it is your own in-effectiveness in dealing with others that makes them difficult?
- Do you have a strong group of supportive people around you?
- Do you attract adversarial relationships?
- Do you feel like the victim, more often than not?

These everyday barometers indicate whether or not you are applying your Emotional Intelligence in your life. They give you an idea of how effectively you are using your emotions, feelings, moods, and those of others as a source of information to help you navigate through life more effectively.

Evidence suggests that applying your Emotional Intelligence will enhance all aspects of your life significantly. Consider briefly the following five factors that make up Emotional Intelligence:

- **Self-Awareness**, or your ability to accurately process information about yourself
- **Mood Management**, or your ability to manage your emotions, rid yourself of bad moods and create positive ones
- **Self-Motivation**, or your ability to persist, overcome frustration, engage in necessary yet boring tasks, initiate productive actions and to cut out counterproductive ones
- **Interpersonal expertise**, or your ability to give and take criticism, work out conflict, build consensus, and develop cooperative relationships
- **Emotional mentoring**, or your ability to respond effectively to the emotions and feelings of others, to help others to solve problems

Each of these factors has an impact on your life. They affect how you parent, how you navigate your relationships or marriage, and they have a significant impact on your work life. Given that we need to use our Emotional Intelligence to succeed in all these areas of our life, it is therefore critical that you develop and apply your Emotional Intelligence in your life.

It is especially important that you learn to apply Emotional Intelligence in your work life, but to neglect any of the other areas of your life would be detrimental, as we see in the example of the CEO in the previous chapter. The first step to applying Emotional Intelligence in your own life involves recognizing the driving emotions in our lives.

The Importance Of Self-Awareness

When asked what the three emotions are that drive what you do every day, it is not surprising that the overwhelming majority of people list anxiety, frustration and fear. When we are anxious or frustrated, this can lead to low levels of productivity at work, and when we are fearful, this leads to tension and conflict on the home front. This is because many people do not have appropriate responses for these emotions, and cannot deal sufficiently and constructively with them.

This has a number of adverse effects, including:

- Weight Gain
- Smoking Far Too Much
- Alcohol and Drug Abuse

It is therefore imperative that you learn to control these emotions, or your response to them, so that you avoid going down the destructive path that is paved with proverbial good intentions.

The good news is this is something that you can learn. You can learn to apply your EI, even though you have never been formally taught how. What you need to do is to consider firstly your inner dialogue, the thoughts that you hold uppermost in your mind. This will influence how you feel and act.

Too many people are not even aware of the dialogue that they have with themselves. So unaware are they of the thoughts that are running through their minds that many of us end up using our own thoughts against us. An increase in self-awareness, particularly of your inner dialogue, can bring you to a point where your thoughts work for you and not against you.

You will start to notice whether you tend to blow things out of proportion, magnifying the significance of a situation. You will also notice if you have the habit of coloring your perceptions of others with negatives; or whether you engage in self-demeaning thoughts and statements.

Being aware of these habits will make you mindful to change them. This will take some time to get used to doing. So why not start right now! Taking even a few minutes a day to really listen to how you talk to yourself is an easy way to increase your awareness of how you talk to yourself and help you develop your EI and apply it!

Managing Your Moods Is Critical!

How many times have you been told to 'snap out of it?' When you're having a bad day, or feeling a little less than chipper, it is the last thing that you want to hear. However, the ability to manage your emotions is a skill that will serve you very well in your pursuit of happiness.

So, how do you 'snap out of it?'

The first step is to understand where your emotion comes from. Being aware of what is going on in your head is a good step to help you identify the root of your mood. What has happened in the recent while that changed your mood, or who 'happened' to you? Why do you feel the way you do about this person or event?

Answering these questions will help you manipulate your mood and replace your 'bad' mood with a 'good' one.

Motivating Yourself!

Self-Motivation is an art. It requires real work, more so than most endeavors that you will undertake in your life. The ability to persist, often in the face of great adversity can take real gumption. Forging your way, often frustratingly through the boring 'must do' tasks on your to do list can be overwhelming.

Are there any ways to make every action a productive one, and to counter unproductive ones, however?

Some actions will take natural priority on your list of things to do. Others however, will not rank highly, but they will be essential if you are to move forward with the task at hand. Think of administration and paperwork, when your primary business is giving helicopter rides. Or even cleaning the kitchen before you can bake that chocolate cake that you have been looking forward to baking all week.

You will need to dig deep within yourself to find the energy and drive for you to accomplish the mundane, so that you can go on and accomplish greater and better things. The old adage, *do what you must so that you can do what you want to*, rings very true here.

We have also all met those people, the ones with great work ethic, who care about quality and are committed to improving themselves, but who rarely get rewarded for their efforts. We have also met their co-worker, the one who is no more hardworking or qualified, but who gets recognition and is often promoted.

Some people just seem to have to work harder for rewards, and no matter how hard they try, they never get past begin. Nothing can be as disheartening as this. Being on the receiving end of this treatment does little to motivate you, especially in the context of a team.

You need to motivate yourself when this happens. You need to go on and get things done, to the best of your ability, regardless of how you feel inside.

Mastering Interpersonal Situations

Applying Emotional Intelligence in your life involves being able to take criticism. You also need to be able to give constructive criticism, without coming across as demeaning or condescending. This is a fine balancing act. You must be able to take it as good as you give it.

Another critical key is being able to work out conflict in an amicable way. This will help you to build consensus and to develop cooperative relationships that work in your personal and in your professional life.

Filtering Emotions

What is the benefit of honing all the above skills? Well, you will develop your ability to respond effectively to the emotions and feelings of others. You will become the go to person when other people need to solve problems.

Whether you need a little bit of brushing up, or you rank way below average and need to work on your EI, now is the best time to do that. There are a number of tests that you can take online that will give you an indication of where you rank in terms of your Emotional Intelligence. You will have seen also that there are a number of offline, real world evaluations that give you an even better idea of how strong you are emotionally!

You will be able to express yourself correctly, to the correct people. You will be able to shift your focus so that you can bring about more empowering emotions in yourself. You will be able to control your impulses and make wise decisions.

Being able to read people's emotional states, you will be able to engage authentically with them. This will allow you to adapt your behavior quickly and easily in any setting that you find yourself in. You will be able to articulate your understanding of other people's perspectives respectfully, so that they feel understood.

You will be able to avoid addictive or destructive behaviors, meaning you will not smoke, or drink too much. And you certainly will not engage in recreational drug use. You will be able to address conflict quickly, and with confidence.

You will be self-motivated, and you will not need deadlines from outside sources to get projects started. In a nutshell, you will be able to leverage social awareness to inspire others positively so that they are consistently authentic in the dealing with you and perform at their best.

So the next time someone's cologne is too strong, or you're tempted to say something 'private' that might be overheard by someone else, or a friend asks for your opinion on a new romantic partner of whom you disapprove, you can apply what you know about EI to any of these situations.

The following chapter deals with just how you can apply your Emotional Intelligence in your dealings with others!

Chapter 7-Using Emotional Intelligence in Your Dealings with Others

We have seen thus far, that one can be born with a high Emotional Intelligence. This is not to suggest however, that it cannot be cultivated. We have also seen that with diligence, and commitment to the process, one can indeed cultivate and grow their Emotional Intelligence.

As daunting as it might seem initially, the exercise of cultivating a high EI is critical. It is important to your overall development as a human being, and it will give you leverage in your pursuit of happiness. You owe it to yourself to invest the time and effort in the development of this critical skill.

When you are confronted with people, one thing is certain. You will be exposed to a wide variety of personalities and emotions. You need to be armed sufficiently with a high enough dose of EI to navigate all these situations well.

When confronted with difficult situations socially, you can benefit from applying your innate Emotional Intelligence to the situation. But even with a lower EI, you can learn from life, and let these experiences teach you what you must, and must not do in various situations.

High EI responses to the situations that follow are suggestions to help you on your way. As you develop your Emotional Intelligence even further though, you will add to these suggestions based on your understanding of how emotions really work in yourself and in other people.

A Rose By Any Other Name!

You find yourself in front of a face that you recognize vaguely. You know that you should know this person, but their name escapes you. You search your brain, trying very hard to remember what the person smiling knowingly at you is called. Try as you might, though, you keep hitting up against brick walls. What do you do?

Well, a high EI response to this situation would not be to avoid this 'unknowing'. You will embarrass the person who has just called you by name and who even wished you well on your upcoming anniversary. They really know you.

The best thing to do in this situation is to make it about yourself. Blaming yourself for not remembering the person's name frees the other person from thinking that they were not memorable enough, and it opens up the conversation for you to be reminded of this lost information. This is a high EI response because it shows consideration for the other person's feelings, and it accepts responsibility for your faux pas.

A Smelly Dilemma!

You find yourself in the presence of somebody who has far too much cologne on. This can be in an elevator, or worse still in a restaurant, or the office. You try to get your mind off it, but the smell fills your nose and your head so that you think that the person has actually bathed in it.

Your hand goes to your nose, although you try to hide this, and you start to sneeze uncontrollably. How do you avoid excusing yourself without leaving the other person feeling awkward?

A low EI response would be to block your nose and point at the culprit. You will want to avoid this, and you definitely want to avoid saying things like 'that's a little too much cologne there buddy', for obvious reasons. The most obvious would be that, like the previous example, you risk embarrassing the other person, who might not even be aware that they have too much cologne on.

A high EI response to this would be again to make it about you. Referring to your allergies is usually a nice way to excuse yourself from the situation and leave everybody feeling 'sorry' for you instead. This shifts the attention to you, and away from the individual, showing concern and empathy for them, which are critical to Emotional Intelligence.

Overheard!

You find yourself with information that you just 'have to share.' It doesn't even matter where you got it. You could have heard it from the proverbial grapevine, or overheard a conversation that was had in private. You could even be the person that this information was shared with 'confidentially'.

You pull a colleague into a toilet cubicle, and you proceed to whisper in hushed tones the dirty little secret that you should not know, and that you have no business sharing anyway. Suddenly the toilet door next to the one you're in opens and somebody rushes out. You've been overheard! How do you handle this?

Well, basically, YOU WILL NOT ENTER INTO SUCH CONVERSATIONS IN THE FIRST PLACE! People with high EIs are able to discern the information that they should and should not share, and they are empathetic to the feelings of other people. Gossiping is one of the first signs that a person has a low level of Emotional Intelligence, actually.

Three's A Crowd!

A friend approaches you excitedly and tells you about the new love of their lives. They might ask you for advice on the best way to proceed with the relationship, because they 'really like this one'. You have your suspicions, and you just don't trust this person. In fact, you hate them. What do you tell your friend so that they do not feel like they should not have told you in the first place, let alone asked for your advice?

Well, a high EI response in this case requires some serious introspection. You need to ask yourself if you are not just feeling insecure that the new love interest will threaten your relationship with your friend. This is the most insightful thing to do before you go ahead and make a fool of yourself, or really risk losing your friend to your own insecurities.

Better Late Than Never!

It is an hour before the beginning of that concert that you could not get tickets to until the last minute, something about someone's grandmother dying so you could have their tickets for a price. Anyway, now you have the tickets, and you decide that going with your best friend might be a good idea.

They've known for a week, so there is no reason for them to be late. But they are, and you're getting impatient. As the seconds tick away on your watch, you call them to no avail, reaching their voicemail. Eventually you have to decide if you will continue to wait for them, or leave them behind. After all, you really want to see this show!

As you enter the concert venue, your phone rings. It is your friend, and you are ready to give them an earful. Do you?

Highly Emotionally Intelligent people will take a few deep breaths. You will give your friend the benefit of the doubt, and allow them to explain why they are not right there pushing through the queue with you. Even if you're the type of person who is never late, your high EI will allow you to put yourself in the other person's shoes, and accept that any number of things could have happened to make them late.

Spinach In Your Teeth!

You are sitting across from somebody at a dinner table and you notice that they have something stuck in their teeth. Or you notice at the office party that Lisa from accounts has lipstick on her teeth. Every part of you wants to point this out. How can you though, and risk embarrassing the person in front of a room full of people?

People with high EIs will evaluate the person, and ask themselves how closely they resemble them. Would you be embarrassed if somebody pointed out to you in public that you had something in your teeth? If so, and if you see yourself in the other person, then you will get them aside and kindly point out the piece of spinach sticking out of their canines.

The list of social interactions that can benefit from your application of Emotional Intelligence can go on and on. EI and its sister, empathy, are essential particularly in service related industries. Considering the fact that a large number of graduate jobs too require you to work as a team, Emotional Intelligence is also of particular importance to these roles.

Understanding what is going on in someone else's mind without them having to tell you is an important skill that you will develop in your pursuit of Emotional Intelligence. You will be able to guess at other people's reactions and build constructive relationships. These are essential for leadership roles and teamwork scenarios.

How To Develop Your Emotional Intelligence?

Take on roles that involve plenty of human interaction. Volunteering is a great place to start, especially if you are working with vulnerable or disabled people on a regular basis. This will allow you to develop empathy, and you will also improve your communication skills. You could also develop this skill as part of a part-time job. But remember, it has to be a job that involves working with other people. These people may be other staff members, or customers. Waiting tables, for instance, is a great part time job that stretches your Emotional Intelligence to its limits.

Getting involved in student societies, sports clubs and drama groups is also a great way to build up this skill. Think of the way emotions can run high in these situations, and how a bit of sensitivity can make the difference between the society working well or failing.

You really can develop your Emotional Intelligence. Sometimes you might need to seek professional advice on how best to deal with people. The same way you pay a personal trainer an exorbitant amount of money a couple of times a week to get you to exercise harder, you can engage the services of an expert to help you learn more about yourself and others. This can go a long way in teaching you how to deal with different types of difficult people.

We cannot expect to just be experts on dealing with other people. We cannot even be expected to be experts when it comes to dealing with our own emotions. This is to be expected though, since we were never formally taught these skills at school. Even college and university do not prepare you for real world interaction with real, dynamic, varying personalities.

It will help you to accept right from the beginning that you will not bring about complete changes in other people, no matter how high your EI is. The good news is, you don't have to. Having increased flexibility and responsiveness in situations is all that is required if you are to make significant improvements in the quality of your life. This is particularly true of work environments and work outputs.

You need to know however that this is very doable. With the right skill and understanding exactly what is needed, you can bring about the changes necessary for you to develop your Emotional Intelligence. Enhancing your EI is the best way to prevent the development of toxic relationships. It also provides you with protection from the damage that toxic people can do to you!

Granted, the above examples might not apply to you. You might never find yourself in these situations. But similar situations arise in our daily lives that require us to apply a measure of Emotional Intelligence. Look around your world, in your daily life, and actively seek out situations that you can apply your EI. You will continue to grow this muscle and develop it until it becomes second nature.

Conclusion

If you want to exert influence in your life and your world, if you want to master conflict resolution, if you want to gain a deeper understanding of other people's perspectives, then Emotional Intelligence is the key that you need to make this possible. You will be able to identify dangerous people or situations before they happen to you, and you will develop a skill for identifying problems before they even begin.

You will greatly decrease your vulnerability in situations where you have to deal with other people. You can also deal better with aggressive behaviors as they show up in your life. These are critical parts of yourself to develop if you are to avoid conflict, or resolve it amicably.

If you find yourself in a position of leadership, Emotional Intelligence will help you to identify suitable managers. You will be able to coach them and bring out the best in them, even if they don't quite believe in themselves just yet. Using your EI, you will also be able to remove managers who behave in a manner that is toxic to the team.

Needless to say, people vary in the levels of understanding that they have for their own feelings. More so, they can be very limited in their understanding of the emotions of others. With conscious effort, however, you can make significant strides in the development and improving of your Emotional Intelligence.

You need to pay attention to your emotional reactions to situations. This is key to developing your personal competence, self-awareness and self-management. You also need to enhance your understanding of why you react this way. Following this, you need to come up with alternative ways of interpreting these situations, and then find constructive ways to deal with the emotional stress that remains.

It is critical that you invest the time required for this introspection. Discuss your findings with people that you trust. Strive to gain an understanding of your emotional reactions and behaviors. You will soon grow in your EI competence.

This process might be expedited by the use of the services of a professional. They can help to speed up the process and help you to identify any problems and obstacles in your way, obstacles that are preventing you from accurately understanding your emotions and your reactions.

Similarly, you can grow your social competence through the same processes. Paying attention to the emotions and behaviors of others, seeking to understand others' behavior through reflection and discussion with third parties, thinking of ways to deal with these situations, and observing the effects of your actions are all part of this process.

It is important for you to understand that you do not need to be directly involved in situations to learn from them either. By simply observing others, and thinking why people behave and react the way they do, seeing which behavior seems helpful in which situations, you can enhance your social competence.

There are psychological issues that could present an enormous barrier to the development of your Emotional Intelligence. Your inner dialogue could feed your limiting beliefs of yourself, or of others. You could have a tendency to interpret situations negatively. This could lead to negative self-fulfilling prophecies.

It could also lead to black and white thinking. This limits your perspective and your openness to other people, especially if those people are criticizing you. If your ways are set in stone, or if you have a rigid personality or thinking patterns, the development of your EI will be stunted.

You might be limited by painful memories as well. This will color your interpretation of present situations, because you will always have an expected negative outcome. You need not let these experiences cloud your interpretation of the current circumstance. These blinkers can block you from learning.

This is where you can use the services of a coaching assistant. If you can afford it, then it is worth the time and investment to get these blinders out of your way. Seek out a coach who is also trained as a therapist. This will stand you in a much better position to overcome your emotional hurdles, and you can then focus on developing your Emotional Intelligence.

In the end, being able to deal with people when they are being rigid or self-centred, aggressive or mean, you will be able to reach your goals.

Therefore, the next time someone asks you what superpower you would most like to have, go ahead and be creative. You know now that Emotional Intelligence is definitely not out of your reach. With a little bit of attention, you can develop your EI muscle until it becomes the backdrop to your new life.

Success is possible in all areas of your life with your new Emotionally Intelligent self. You will enjoy better relationships, at work and in your private life, as well as an improvement in all your endeavors. Simply developing your understanding of how you operate on an emotional level, as well as the emotional motivators of other people, you will be well on your way to living the life of your dreams.

Having a very high IQ is no guarantee that you will succeed in life. In fact, many people with impressive IQs live less than fantastic lives. They are reclusive, and troubled, seemingly overwhelmed by the massive amount of grey matter they have between the ears. What has been missing, until now, has been an understanding of how to manage your EI, and marry it successfully with your IQ.

It can be argued in fact, that having a high EI stands you in much better stead for great achievement. Understanding how to manipulate emotions within yourself and others can be far more effective than doing well academically. This can be seen in the blatantly obvious discrepancy between those with many qualifications, and those who do well financially and generally. Bill Gates did not graduate from college. Neither did many of the ridiculously wealthy and happy people you read about every day. Richard Branson grew up with learning difficulties. In fact, he is dyslexic. We can go on and on, but this is not necessary.

Granted, some of these names conjure up images of intellectuals with glasses, and grey suits (yes, I'm talking about Bill Gates), and it is true that some of these men have got a significant amount of grey matter. Fortunately, this is not a precursor to the success that they have enjoyed. A significant part of their achievement was because of their high Emotional Intelligence.

From just the few examples above, you can see that people with higher EIs do far better than their contemporaries with lower EIs, even though they might have very average IQs. A high

Emotional Intelligence is therefore a critical skill to have today.

And it is a skill. While some people are naturally predisposed to a higher Emotional Intelligence, you can develop this intelligence, as the preceding chapters have indicated. The suggested ways to improve your Emotional Intelligence are not merely guidelines. They are steps that you can start taking today to change your life, and to give you a much better chance at succeeding at everything that you do.

Human beings are complex creatures. It is therefore understandable that we would have multiple intelligences that we can tap into as is needed. Granted, these intelligences are not created equal, and while you might have a high dose of one, it is not guaranteed that you will score highly across all of them. What you can do however, is to apply yourself in the development of these intelligences until you reach your true potential.

Potential is a great thing to waste. Revisit the chapters in this book to gain mastery over your emotions, and work steadily towards the development of your EI. Countless researchers have stated that your level of Emotional Intelligence is the number one predictor of personal and professional success. You will navigate through life with much greater ease the higher your EI is.

You will benefit across the following areas in your life:

- You will be able to control your temper and be less impulsive
- You will be able to cope effectively with stress
- You will be able to confidently stand up for yourself
- You will be able to articulate your discomfort
- You will be able to set clear boundaries for yourself
- You will experience increased positivity

- You will be able to get and stay motivated
- You will be able to make better decisions
- You will be able to influence other people positively
- You will be able to interact better with other people
- You will develop emotional resilience

The list of benefits is endless. You will enjoy these benefits in your personal and professional life. Regardless of what you have been through in the past, and no matter the mistakes you have made up until right now, start right now to cultivate a higher Emotional Intelligence. No matter where you are in your life, you can begin building you EI today, and start to reap the rewards.